Assembled In Britain

Assembled in Britain

Poems so far 1972–1986

Stewart Henderson

Marshall Pickering

Cover design by Paul Edwards, Angle Studios
Back cover photograph by Douglas Unwin

Marshall Morgan and Scott
Marshall Pickering
3 Beggarwood Lane, Basingstoke, Hants RG23 7LP, UK

Copyright © 1986 By Stewart Henderson
First published in 1986 by Marshall Morgan and
Scott Publications Ltd
Part of the Marshall Pickering Holdings Group
A subsidiary of the Zondervan Corporation

British Library CIP Data

Henderson, Stewart
    Assembled in Britain: poems so far
    1972-1986
    I. Title
    821'.914   PR6058.E49/

    ISBN 0-551-01374-5

Text Typeset in Century Textbook by
Brian Robinson, Buckingham
Printed in Great Britain by Hazell Watson & Viney Ltd,
Member of the BPCC Group,
Aylesbury, Bucks

To my darling Carol

I can never thank you enough
for the richness of your heart
and your enduring love.
This is your book

Acknowledgements

The 'From a Nightmare' poems were first published in
Whose Idea of Fun is a Nightmare? by MGO
The 'Fan Male' sequence first appeared in the limited
edition, Fan Male, published by Stride Publications

Several of the poems in this book came into being
through commissions, including:

'Yule Gruel', and 'African Fruit' for Tear Fund
'For Valeri And His Kind' for The Jubilee Campaign
'Madeline' was first published in '100 Contemporary
    Christian Poets' by Lion
'Food Parcel' for BBC Television
'An Arrest' for BBC Radio 1

To these organisations, and the many other radio
stations and magazines that have been kind enough
to feature my work, I offer my grateful thanks.

Contents

New Stuff

From A Nightmare
(1972—1975)

Hanging Around

A pair of rubber gloves picked me up
and allowed me to dangle
by my ankles
I swayed like an unpeeled banana
and was then slapped in a most peculiar place
(my mother told me)
so as life's breath
could slowly slither into my jelly lungs
I gave a completely convincing performance
of confusion, agony and terror
Now when gangsters saying they are people
spike me with their looks
or shoot dumdum bullet shaped words
into my body
which explode inside and make rather a mess
though they don't leave a mark on my face
I feel again I'm swaying in space
and being slapped in a most peculiar place.

Mind the Doors

The tube, the whole tube and nothing but the tube

A man, not aware of madness,
wandered into the rush hour
holding a red carnation.
He boarded the train
and hunched himself around the flower
like a cloud.
'What redness, what perfection' he praised
fondling the bud delicately to his tired mackintosh
the train panted along in numerical sequence
    1234   1234   1234   1234
Businessmen, weary after a hard day's lusting at the
    office
and office girls their nails chipped and tights torn
got in and out of compartments like clockwork cattle
and soon there were many
all knowing what it felt like to be toothpaste
The man tried to protect his flower
but people blew smoke rings that spelt couldn't care
    less
as the carnation gasped for breath
amidst the crush it was crushed
and the man whimpered his way off the train
passengers giggled their way past him
as he sat on the stairs outside the station
with sellotape and sorrow in his hand
trying to repair his little piece of God.

Poem for Big Al

On the day that Solzhenitsyn discovered
that truth had finally been raped to death
I was writing a letter to the manufacturers
to tell them my pipe had got woodworm
and please could I have my money back.
When he sat alone in his Moscow flat
listening to his own breathing and waiting for
    footsteps
I was annoyed
because I'd bought a carton of cream that was two
    days old
and I couldn't make myself a decent Gaelic coffee.
Whilst the K.G.B. were doing a brilliant impression
of the hound of the Baskervilles
I was checking the bill suspiciously
in a cheap curry house
see pilau rice's gone up another five pence.
On the day
that freedom was dragged
naked and bleeding through Red Square
I pulled faces at God
Cause it was raining again.

Yours, Not Ours

You are as inevitable as morning
and you are there
long before the first Woodbine croak is heard
at the bleary eyed bus stops of the city.
You watch and wonder
as the sound of waking
mumbles its chorus across roof tops
You see and hear lovers readjust their dreams
in the not quite right of day
You listen to the out of tune clatter of newspapers
drowning out the concert pitch spot-on of the trees
This is a tired morning, as street sweepers clock on
We have stolen it from you
and fashioned it in our own image
You have not yet charged us with theft
and when you do
our defence will be inadequate
the dog ends in the gutter have no apologies
    written on them
there are no acknowledgements in the personal
    columns
the milk bottles hold no thank you notes
and the morning yawns steadily onwards
the morning that is not ours
but always yours.

Splintered Messiah

I don't want a splintered Messiah
in a sweat stained greasy grey robe
I want a new one
I couldn't take this one to parties
people would say 'who's your friend?'
I'd give an embarrassed giggle and change the
 subject
If I took him home
I'd have to bandage his hands
The neighbours would think he's a football hooligan
I don't want his cross in the hall
it doesn't go with the wallpaper
I don't want him standing there
like a sad ballet dancer with holes in his tights
I want a different Messiah
streamlined and inoffensive
I want one from a catalogue
who's as quiet as a monastery
I want a package tour Messiah
not one who takes me to Golgotha
I want a King of Kings
with blow waves in his hair
I don't want the true Christ
I wanna false one.

Who Never Gets in the New Year's Honours List?

Whose idea of fun is a nightmare?
Who invented holiday camps
then sent Adolf a five year lease?
Who giggles like a child
when death is mentioned?
Who giggles like death when a child is mentioned?
Who sent Caiaphas an estimate for the cross?
Who made the ouija board just another party game?
Who tried to put God out of a job?
Who whistles 'If I ruled the world'
then makes everything go black?

Crack Rap Snap

Centre of Londonderry, October 1974, about 8.00 pm

Between the crack, rap, snap of a rifle shot
and the before-falling bullet-bound body
there was a space
I had two alternatives, a numbness
or the thought of a car backfiring.
If it was the former it wasn't true,
it's that Reginald Bosanquet's fault
with his vivid imagination,
Oh God turn over to 'Z Cars'
before I believe him.
If it was the latter then there's a hole in the exhaust.
Went on, read me poems,
got laughs where people were supposed to laugh,
Came off, got changed,
Soldier shot
signed a few autographs
through the head
felt pleased
dead
Road blocks on the way out of Derry
and the rain's dressed for a funeral,
crying down the windscreen.

Messianic Blues

What kind of Saviour?
a soft shoe shuffle
hair never ruffled
chocolate truffle Saviour
a finger in the air
stickers everywhere Saviour
a neat
sweet
petit
graffiti Saviour
a monopolised
before your eyes
compromising Saviour
a cure your back ache
wrapped in soap flakes
explodes from huge birthday cakes Saviour
a Stars on Sunday
have your own way
a dressed in drag
drives a jag
a left wing right wing
centre forward
upside down
wrong way round
3p a pound
a half day closing
always dozing Saviour
A carpenter from Galilee
who simply said
Follow me . . . Saviour

Fan Male

(1976—1983)

The Last Communion

(Sir John Betjeman 1906–1984)

When dinner in Bagshot cost less than a quid
And sex was a thing that the foreigners did
When Rayners Lane station was dreamy with steam
And never a Walkman in Highbury was seen

Those chewable flapjacks with whizzo cream teas
And soul tearing glimpses of tweedy girls' knees
A swift set of tennis in Home Counties light
You wearing khaki whilst she was in white

When salesmen were breeding in mock tudor bars
And churches were free from the plunk of guitars
When abbeys were blest to seat ladies in lace
And bishops assured them that God knew his place

When Jesus was mystery instead of a friend
A shroud must have seemed a logical end
And the Prayer Book declares the dead will be raised
But the sky above Cornwall's been weeping for days.

Jerusalem

She barely sleeps
she counts her children nightly
tonight they are all there
tomorrow she may wail
A body,
like a fiercely thrown tennis ball,
may pound off a wall somewhere
She will bury another
her hands again will arch in grief
over her trembling eyes
her birds will choose
the lowest boughs
and remain silent
She counts her children nightly

Surrey Postcards (Part I)

Our Garden, Outside the Back Door

A grounded squirrel
ears taut for the sound of stiffening cats
delicately disrobes an acorn
like a deb removing evening gloves

On the Road Between Esher and Cobham

The rain is celebrating something
clattering through the branches
trampolining off the cats eyes

Marley's Pond in February

Beneath the gloomy ice
Goldfish flash in and out of view
like belisha beacons in fog

*Oxshott Woods, Autumn Early Evening
After a Hailstorm*

Blake has been sketching the sky
It is now an astral bougainvillea
Holding even deeper mysteries

Gutterpress Erotica

gutterpress erotica gutterpress erotica
Sonia's twenty-one, comes from Canvey Island
Likes fast cars, cor dig those hubs,
And wants to visit Thailand

gutterpress erotica gutterpress erotica

Wait and see who will it be
Page three thumbed in expectancy
Pouting girls with tumbling curls
All in the cause of

gutterpress erotica gutterpress erotica

Some believe in feminism
some stand up for liberalism
some are into self respect
for every living organism
some say that Vanessa's right
and raise their fists for Trotskyism
but most men most men most men like
most men like a
most men like a bit
most men like a bit of

gutterpress erotica gutterpress erotica

And it's three lines for the Afghans
as they face extermination
A paragraph for Thatcher
and her struggles with inflation
And not a single comma on that boring Polish crisis
But Sonia's chest gets one whole page
Oh by the way she's Pisces

gutterpress erotica gutterpress erotica

pressica erotigut guttica erotipress gutterpress erotica

And If It Be Right

And if it be right
that love is a leaf
then I picked you in Spring
when your veins stood out
and your greenness was susceptible
to the cynical frost

And if it be right
that love is a leaf
then sometimes
I am the cause of Autumn
I blow the selfish wind
I spit the rain that chills
to bring the brittle brownness

And if it be right
that love is a leaf
then Summer is truly ours
when you shine like the grass
and turn
in gentle yearning to the sun

Went to . . .

Went to Rome once
Saw the Colosseum
Now inhabited by numerous stray cats
Imagined cruel Emperors, savage crowds,
howling relatives, bigger cats
and inwardly retched.
Also saw a red haired Chinaman
and a one legged Italian riding a bike.

Went to Munich once
Glorious city
Thought about the inevitable,
articulate bully boys
leading a nation into mayhem
watched them striding through
the stirring crowds.
Thought about visiting Dachau
but inspected my own soul instead.

Went to Paris once
Didn't bother with Notre Dame
as I'd seen the film.
Strange flippant city
Not a place to think in.

Went to Jerusalem once
Could have sworn I smelt heaven
several times
Watched the Crucifixion
Actually volunteered to hold the nails
as he was roped on to the cross.
Got spat at by a camel
Funny how animals sense things.

Surrey Postcards (Part II)

Watching the Races from Esher Station

Stretching steaming straining horses
Lapsed Pegasus'
Awaiting the rightful return of their wings

Oxshott Woods, November Afternoon

A gun shot tattoos the stark air
Grieved rabbits prepare for a wake
And the trees stand sullen and disapproving

Scilly Isles Roundabout

The clouds are pink and puffy eyed
in the morning rush hour sky

The White Swan at Thames Ditton, Summer Morning

Loud ducks with flat wet heads
like spivs in black out pubs
roll and clamour past prospective clients

An Anti-Jewish Evangelical Writes a Sort of Sonnet

Gentile Jesus meek and mild
Somehow allowed to be defiled
By taking on a Jewish frame
A Jewish heart, a Jewish name
Gentile Jesus meek and mild
Why were you born a Jewish child?
Gentile Jesus meek and mild
It really gets me rather riled
That under Jahweh's supervision
Your body suffered circumcision
Gentile Jesus out of place
In such a foul obnoxious race
We pray become the perfect man
Confirm yourself an Ang-li-can

Royal Baby

Funny the way some kings are born
Amidst lip bitten crowds hushed bunting
and big eyed television cameras
The proclamation as Sainsbury champagne corks
ricochet off clouds
Video king of a bleak and techno land
The rattling natter of journalists
parrots with press cards
as crimplene ladies with stout forearms
and gold wrist watches beam happily,
catalogue angels on rent rebates

And then there was the man with pebble glasses
    and green teeth
One handled grimy tartan shopping bag
full of mallets and bread knives
as the crowd murmured appreciation for quick
    thinking policemen
probably end up as a headline somewhere
'Nutter nailed at Royal Rave up'

Funny the way some kings are born

Funny the way some kings are born
three strange visitors on camels
bring seemingly impractical gifts
as the smell of animal dung
seeps and creeps out into the sharp black night

the breath of God lies kicking in straw
whilst outside
the man with pebble glasses and green teeth
sniggers to the sheep
'He's a bastard you know'

Funny the way some kings are born

I Once Was a Tree

I once was a tree
in a field I stood

I once was a tree
each spring I would bud

I once was a tree
and my leaves were fair

I once was a tree
as they kissed the air

I once was a tree
oh that deathly sound

I once was a tree
as I wept to the ground

A tree I once was
the saw was wiped clean

I'm now centre spread
in a porn magazine

Madeline

Madeline are you tired of the jokes
The   knock knock   who's there
lesbian   lesbian who   lesbeavinyou.
Don't worry Madeline,
They're usually told by people frightened
of their own sexuality.
I've given up counting your tears Madeline.
Your eyes confused and unsure,
Your face preparing itself for despair.
Your heart full of empty passion and dreary rooms
Your heart like a nervous sparrow fearing winter
You have considered death but found it too severe,
and life is now an endless sad humming.
Madeline, come back from the past,
retreat from that bruised childhood.
Madeline, come out of the closet
and go to your true lover.
Go to him Madeline
He's waiting for you
The candles are lit,
an angel tasted the wine and went off dancing
Go to him Madeline
your healing is in him,
go and be a woman for the Son of Man.

Surrey Postcards (Part III)

Esher Golf Course

Crows, idling amongst
the black brittle branches
laughing at their own jokes

Milbourn's Pond, Late Evening

It gleams like a spit and polished shoe
A moor hen sprints across the water
scuffing the surface

Richmond Bridge, Early Monday Morning

Two swans on their way back from paradise
meander down river
away from the ragged traffic

An Arrest

Last night Father Christmas was arrested
He was detained by the S.P.G.
for causing a riotous assembly, a fracas,
a public disturbance, an etcetera.
Also apprehended were several goblins,
numerous creatures with bells on their heads
pointed feet and green hair
These characters were later identified by the
    authorities
as probable illegal immigrants.
A reindeer was also taken into custody
for driving a sleigh with a bald hoof.
The Police State
that Christmas was under close surveillance for
    several minutes
as were his accomplices
The accused was seen in Oxford Street
banging tambourines, lampposts
and sometimes each other
and dancing steps never seen before.
Christmas, the police went on,
was by this time
emerging as the ring leader
he pushed into bus queues
and was seen to entice
disgruntled shoppers dreaming of hot baths
jaded bank clerks knee deep in mince pies
and innocent children to partake in the senseless
    anarchy.
A display of this sort by a fat red man
who claims he hails from the planet of stars

has caused penetrating questions to be asked in
  the House
but as usual nobody has come up with an answer.
Draped, robed and caressed in tinsel
Father Christmas, alias Santa Claus
was bundled into the back of a squad car
his cheeks like fire engines glowing in the neon
  evening.
The police confirmed that no illegal substances
were found in his possession
however it was noticed
he smelt strongly of snow and wood smoke.
When charged Christmas pleaded guilty
to an outbreak
of spontaneous joy.
Asked if he had anything further to add
he chuckled with child-like glee and said
"Bethlehem, Bethlehem,
the joy, the joy of Bethlehem."

Richard Wurmbrand

I only met him once
his long body
curved and delicate
like a well sucked wishbone
and behind his eyes
the memories of countless nights
manacled to the nightmares of Satan
his ears besieged by devilish anthems
declaring that his Christ was dead
And now every movement
magnifying the taut weariness
of a prisoner of war
a walking twig
a victim of the fight
between heaven and hell
his body like his Messiah's
so gladly given to torture
for the sake of strange mystical things
like resurrections and kneeling with angels
to sing the joyous symphonies of paradise
I only met him once
and I walked away and wept

We Were Going to be Twins

What attracted us to one another initially
was we shared the same womb
albeit the unconsidered products of flippant passion
Anyway, we were pre-natal room mates
checking each other's progress
transfixed by the budding of tiny fingernails
and the rhythm of miniscule chests
rising and falling like pale pink bellows
My brother, for that's what he was now becoming,
had a curious almost whimsical shape
his head leaning to one side
as if he were always about to ask a question
He used to poke gentle fun
at my by now rapidly expanding feet
I only had two
but on occasions because of the space they took up
they seemed to number far more
I can't remember exactly when we were terminated
My brother went first
in plunged a knife
ended his life
with a slish and a slash and a silent scream
I proved to be a more unwilling participant
like an irritating piece of dust
in the very corner of a skirting board
a long thin nozzle entered my sanctuary/death cell
and I was sucked into oblivion
along with bits of my brother
all courtesy of the National Health Service
In California some beloved dogs
when they expire
are buried in oak coffins with gold handles

Respectful mourners attend and weep accordingly
We were poured into a black plastic sack
not a hymn nor a prayer was heard
We were going to be twins
my brother and I

Two Liverpool Nursery Rhymes and a Limerick

Two Liverpool Nursery Rhymes

Henry the Hog went walking his dog
Through Sefton Park one day
He met a cat called Fancy That
Who was out on bail

*   *   *

The Anfield Gink
Is coloured pink
And likes to bathe in the kitchen sink
But when the water's far too hot
He crosses his eyes and shouts a lot

Creation Limerick

Adam and Eve didn't bother with diets
And they neither got fatter nor thinner
Then their dreadful mistake
Of believing a snake
Made them fully clothed weight watching sinners

The Writes of Love
(1972—1986)

I fell in love on a Thursday
When the streets were grim with rain
I should have concocted
A site more exotic
Like a blurred lens
besotted
On the banks of the Seine

But we're not that struck on epics
With intruding violins
Love is you
your caresses
your flower print dresses
and a clip round the ear
when I make the tea strong

*　　*　　*

Loving you is like
kissing an angel's ankle
Being with you
one step nearer
the Temple

*　　*　　*

She now has eyes
where there used to be deserts
And even sandstorms
are now
too occasional
to notice

For we will not walk
like shadows
Afraid, not knowing Light
We will together
in radiance not found
on this black, racked planet
walk with steps already trod
Not by us, but for us

*　　*　　*

The swing happy day
When you said yes
And the sun beamed
for hours
As the breath of
the heavens
Trailed a
bouquet of glowing
And the Maker of men
granted joy for my counsel
and
peace through
your troth

*　　*　　*

Eight rhymes with date
which recalls 22nd December
rhymes with remember
which is too happy
to bother scanning
that dizzyjoy day
rhymes with may I
make you my wife
rhymes with life of
mine given to thee
so that
we may complete the
earthly vows
commissioned in heaven

        *   *   *

You come as lonely
set apart
with facets others don't possess
You are
the sound of flowers
on an anxious morning

        *   *   *

If music be the food of love
Then you to me are concert pitch

        *   *   *

I'm as thrilled as a cat
munching on beef
I'm plodging around
and counting my teeth
All because
You're back with me

        *   *   *

Within the inextinguishable light
and power
that is our love
amidst
New joys of tenderness
and the promise
of eternal mornings
spent in glory
This is the essence
of what we build
From the source of love
I give you love, my love.

*   *   *

I adore thee more
than the vaults of light
O creature of hope
O anthem to God
And I love thee more
because of thy light
O scarred
and singing beauty

We will write
in the language
of infinite love
The sky will be our paper
the stars
our pen
O come that day,
come now.

New Stuff

Food Parcel

Snapped and splintered He was
to be then distributed in celebration
Edible confetti
hurled against the breeze of His Father's creation

Hoist upon a Roman meat hook He was
left to shrivel in the roaring sun
Like a random downpour of dripping javelins
scars flew across His flesh
This process was meant to cure Him
but it was the red rain of His falling blood
that cured you

Mocked and taunted He was
yelled at, beaten
Requested to repeat the loaves and fishes caper
with an assurance of a bigger crowd if He did

Gathered up later He was
it seemed there was too much of Him
His body became the leftovers
to be wrapped and packed tenderly
into a pedal bin tomb
But there the burial became a cremation
as the Son of God burned death to a cinder

And out of it He came
so that you can feast
And now begin again

African Fruit

African fruit   African fruit
Plucked from plantations
Dispersed to the nations
Exotic exports leave behind the privations
African fruit   African fruit
Wrenched from the root African fruit

African fruit skin blotched and sagging
Hanging at half mast
See how they prosper
Flies and mosquitos

Diamonds in Sloane Street coffee in Weybridge
Grapefruit in Sainsbury's African fruit

Bald adolescents virility shrunken
Parched breasts are cracking empty and swaying
Wrenched from her root African fruit

Cashews in Putney   lemons in cocktails
Mahogany Hampstead African fruit
Vultures like dustmen   African fruit
Collecting the wastage   African fruit
Rulers drink whisky   African fruit
Mothers are weeping   African fruit
God weeps the longest African fruit

Bulbous eyed babies glowing like coffins
Corpses are snowflakes each one is different

How much is left?
How much is left?
How much is left of God's African fruit?

What If One Day

What if one day God forsook love and logic
and declared that He has a tendency to lie
depending on His mood?
Faith in Him would equal
an ecclesiastical russian roulette
As we lay in the darkening shadows of intensive
    care
would we gladly anticipate this sadistic after life
    dare
or, frantically prised out of some motorway carnage
or, less hideously, one day left to slide down a bus
    stop
like an expiring marionette,
would we be prepared for cosmic bingo
our souls the lucky numbers?

What if one day God got bored with compassion
with no rules to explain his behaviour
because He decided such things were restricting
and hence obsolete
At our death we would fully inherit eternal life
But then again, we might not
because there was an R in the month.

What if God
treated our trust
the way we treat His infinite love
contemptuously
and lacking commitment?

It All Started At School

It all started at school
the daydreaming I mean
lots of time for it there
especially during Maths
all manner of fantasies
Footballer, adoring crowds
gleaming boots, neatly tied
Inspected my body
discovered I was knock-kneed, bow legged
and pigeon toed
and my father was a policeman
Captain of a Whaling boat
racing through thundering oceans
in search of the fearsome beast
Arrived home to find my goldfish had died
wept ceaselessly
could never do that to a whale
besides, his mates may come and get me
Spy, looking sinister in East Berlin
passing slim envelopes to thick set men
no chance, never went to Cambridge.
I still dream
Poet,
clever stanzas, well timed jokes
intense lyrical visions
poet . . . perhaps, someday.

Kidstuff

When I was a child
I could never see the point of the heroine
She was always feeble
She screamed a lot
She got captured
And was taken to a very high tower
Someone always came in the end

When I was a child
Someone made me see the point of heroin
I was always feeble
I scream a lot
I got captured
I'm in a high tower
Someone may come in the end

The Teddy Bear

The teddy bear was reported unhurt
a few grazes
a dazed look
but otherwise nothing serious.
Nobody's told teddy that tonight
he'll be sleeping alone
he will not feel
a warm biscuit crumb milk breath on his face
or have stories
of dark monsters and luscious heroes read to him.
In time
he'll miss being picked up by the ear
and thrown against the wall
when gymslip tempers were bright and fuming.
He will now have to wash his own face
and feed himself
but God knows how
And every Sunday
after confession or morning service
he will take colourless flowers to the grave
and smile an unfunny smile
at the headstone
'Yo ho ho, let's keep mum
and forget about Ulster 'til Kingdom come'

We Used to Call it Running

We used to call it running
There on Crosby Beach
As the reek
from the oozing oil stained sand
would sometimes make us reach
And our plimsolls
would stink for days and days
From running on Crosby Beach

And I would wear my big brother's shorts
And a basketball singlet
with the number torn off
We'd sprint and then wheeze
And sweat like the sun
Nearly nineteen with a smoker's cough
There on Crosby Beach

But now it's called jogging
And one must look right
Immaculate tracksuited exorcism
For those who spend
their lunchtimes getting tight
Before fashion and fear of death
Started to screech
It was once called running
On Crosby Beach

Definition of a Poet—
Word Processor

In my fast forward user friendly Utopia
variety would be endless
a laser digital watch that gives the weather
    forecast in Japanese
totally useless but very impressive
a quadrophonic five year memory video recorder
    that not only records
programmes off my own TV but also the chap's
    next door
In my cursor to home nirvana
God would be a redundant word used only by
    monks and maniacs
Nature would be improved
by the sound of disk driven synthesized bird song
Monday would be blackbirds to enhance the
    romantic in me
Tuesday nightingales to bring out the romantic
    in me
And Wednesday, Thursday and Friday
would be the low clacking of a blood gargling
    vulture
to illustrate the me in me
Oh come with me to that dry ice erase to end of
    line valhalla
forsake the print out that once was you
fall to your knees and shout in a loud voice
yea to the microwave oven
repeat in unison
I once was lost but now I've got a sonar powered
    kettle
that plays tea for two as it comes up to the boil

Brothers and sisters what shall you do to inherit
  Eternal life,
Interface together and believe on the Grand Master
  Trio
Password, keystrokes and VDU
Allow our counsellors
to escort you into paradise
where nothing will perish but your heart

A Prophet and a Wet Thursday

On sombre afternoons such as these
when trees huddle
as if expecting the moon
to wander amongst them
Isaiah paces the dripping grass
addressing the limp washing line
prophesying to the grumbling sky
Leaves dip and strain
to get a better view
as the anguished evening approaches
Only the humble
hear his message

Today Caring was Rediscovered

This morning after the rain had tea broke
I saw an old lady drying the grass with a towel
not wishing to embarrass her
I watched this tender action from a distance
the birds who had previously been sheltering
under leaking leaves
shook their feathers and peered out,
casting inquisitive looks to each other
'Who is this strange disciple of nature?'
they thought
'with her back bent and her knees damp'
The old lady continued to caress each blade
as if it were a longago lover she had left
in the attic
The birds who were by now overjoyed
began to sing
but it wasn't a song I had heard before
not a song for insensitive lovers on their way
    home
from an all night party
or small children with bald fathers
in parks on summer mornings
but a song of beauty
and by now people had gathered
around the old lady
they lifted their ears above their heads
and were amazed by the beauty of the song
And soon reporters arrived
with headlines and biros that leaked dishonesty
all wanting to know where this beautiful song had
    come from
'It must be the birds' said a young executive

65

And then, as everyone waved their cheque books and
promised incorrect truths
the birds stopped singing
and turned their backs on the huge crowd
leaving the advertisers, the sightseers, the ice
   cream man
with a vision of failed exploitation
So they drifted, drifted, drifted away
without ever noticing the old lady
drying the grass with a towel.

Behind the Wire

We are in the lame room
the lame room
the lame room
we are in the lame room
for we've done something wrong

They are in the same room
the same room
the same room
they are in the same room
for they've said something wrong

We have murdered, pimped and stolen
lied until our lips have swollen
ours is not a nice tune
where else do we belong?

They all daydream in this nightmare
of a God Who really does care
this is not a sane room
where else do they belong?

When we reach the end room
the dead room
the doom room
when we reach the last room
will there be room for us?

they don't fear the dead room
the dull room
the skull room
they don't fear the last room
for they've done nothing room

Galilee

Whisper now sweet lake
neglect the tender shore
and leave the bleached hills to the sun
I need the wisdom of dusk
when birds confer
and cows suck the pitiful grass
In your colour
almost silver now
as if the stars had dropped
and immersed themselves
in the beauty of your lapping
is the acuteness of truth
As on your waters
much madness ago
came One Who braced your rebellious waves
Tell me, what was He like?
did His feet glisten with the kisses of God?
Whisper now sweet lake
I fear a storm of doubt in me

Raison d'Etre

The hairs on our heads have been numbered
Our fingerprints
prove we're unique
And though science and surgeons
Could scoop out our hearts
That still couldn't remove the mystique
Of being made something from nothing
And given the jewel of free will
To love or abstain
To sin or refrain
To cartwheel through life
Or sit still

The Last Enemy

And He Who each day
reveals a new masterpiece of sky
and Whose joy
can be seen in the eyelash of a child
Who when He hears of our smug indifference
can whisper an ocean into lashing fury
and talk tigers into padding roars
This my God
Whose breath is in the wings of eagles
Whose power is etched in the crags of mountains
It is He Whom I will meet
in Whose Presence I will find tulips and clouds
kneeling martyrs and trees
the whole vast praising of His endless creation
And He will grant the uniqueness
that eluded me
in my earthly bartering with Satan
That day when He will erase the painful gasps of
    my ego
and I will sink my face into the wonder of His
    glorylove
and I will watch planets converse with sparrows
On that day
when death is finally dead

Moderate Despair

I've almost finished with England
With Angela Rippon and riots
As I pay for my video nasty
And stick to my F plan diets

I'll throw in the towel with Britannia
As soon as my giro comes through
And to complete my isolation
I'll change my religion to Jew

I'm not that fond of Great Britain
It's either too blue or too red
I looked at the sleeping pills longingly
But voted Alliance instead

Someone's Mother in a Funeral Parlour

Lovely she was
not a fresh firm peach of leggy youth
but stately
her sinewy skin beginning to droop
from her lace dainty forearms
lovely she was

Laid out she was
the glad sheen of death
glazing her wisp girlish face
presented for eternity in white
she thought white a bit common
Soon to awake from the dark night of life
lovely she was

Approaching the Finish

So now I try to discuss the end times
as we plod through the suburbs of Armageddon
And will we glance the Anti-Christ
cruising past in a taxi
Will he be elected democratically
Will he kiss babies' heads
Be given government approval
What shape is he
Could it really be that nice United Nations
Will he lullaby us in the apathy of our own living
  rooms
Will his intrusion be courtesy of BBC 2
Will he have a nice line in deprecating humour
Kind eyes that spell peace
With a heart full of death camps

So now I dare to discuss the end times
What point in a venemous creature
That claws and rips indiscriminately
Why not one that is amongst us, amenable,
  approachable
Like the family alsatian with a lolloping tongue
rising from his rug in the corner
forsaking his rubber bone
and, mad with snarls,
to ravage a passing infant

So now I fear to discuss the end times
This enemy that Daniel gasped
That may be about to come
In a mannish form or a country or an ideology
This enemy that retches at the sight of an empty tomb

How we need to be in Truth
for fear of inviting him to dinner
discussing him affectionately over cocktails
becoming angry when people slight him
And what do we do when he performs miracles
heals the sick
as we stand perplexed and fearful
And if we are not based in truth
We will embrace deception
He will become the Maypole
And we will dance around him
Our brains full of evil bells
Our future crammed with sulphurous smells
How we need to love the Truth.

Dark Peace

(Why aren't holy men whole any more?)

This is a dark peace
Where priests despise You
And fondle our babes

This is a dark peace
Where bishops scold You
And read to us a deviant lesson

This is a dark peace
Where the breath of death
Is to many the kiss of life

This is a dark peace
Where the judges of paradise
Dangle like naked lightbulbs from ceilings
And few have heard
The terrifying quietness of You

Soon You will speak
Into this dark peace

My Heart Had a Riot on Waterloo Station

My heart had a riot on Waterloo Station
like an empty bellied tigress
it was not aware of reason
it threw bricks at the toilets
and screamed 'liar' at the departure board
it butted a passing nun
'Single to Hampton Court, please. Thank you'
my heart had a riot on Waterloo Station
it writhed on the concourse
roaring 'you're all to blame'
it shuffled up to winos and demanded money
it kicked hobbling pigeons
'New Statesman and the Standard, please. Thank you'
my heart had a riot on Waterloo Station
it called white passengers racists
and black ticket collectors niggers
it told lewd jokes to career girls with briefcases
it got off at Wimbledon
and swore at the platform
'Mars bar and a packet of Polos, please. Thank you'
my heart had a riot on Waterloo Station
it took off its tie and strangled a cocksure
    adolescent
threw punches at loud football supporters
bellowing 'this is vengeance'
it wept
it gnawed itself
it became fearful and conciliatory
my heart had a riot on Waterloo Station
next Sunday my heart will be in church
chasing forgiveness

Pentecost is Every Day

I share and share and share again
sometimes with a new language
which, if you are so open
will take you behind the sky
and award you cartwheels across the sun
I give and give and give again
not restricted by the church calendar
or concocted ritual
I have no need of anniversaries
for I have always been
I speak and speak and speak again
with the sting of purity
that can only be Me
causing joyous earthquakes in the mourning soul
   of man
I am and am and am again

On Falling in Love

Approach it properly
don't go daft over lipstick
or the way
the body shapes itself in certain places
Refrain from finding your belle
then imagining her
bikini clad with seductive lips
offering you a martini
on an isolated beach in the Caribbean
this is known as fantasy
which is famous for its short term attractions
and will cause you to go out
and find another advert
Fall in love with the person
the skin, the teeth, the hair
get to know her giggle
the way she holds a cup of coffee
Love without walls
Approach it properly

Gift

(To Edward)

This child
a helpless jewel of creation
more cherished by Him
than the praising skies of morning

This child
toes and eyelashes
formed by Him
Who tossed stars seemingly at random
and made oceans deeper than joy

This child
first glimpsed
by His eyes of Infinite Love
first caressed
by His hands of Endless Truth

This child
a heavenly anthem
that kicks the worship rhythms
of the unheard choirs of paradise

This child
given by Him Who was
and is
and is to come

Stable as a Rock

Soon the perfect pitch of heaven
will be just a fragile yell
slithering through the maiden's moisture
past the howling hounds of hell

Oh majestic contradiction
of a virgin's milk filled breast
nourishing Creation's owner,
now a kicking, lowly guest

Such a presence, it would blind you,
is confined to flesh and blood
tiny hands grasp at the darkness
searching for the deathly wood

As the demons seek to ambush
such a small and frail Messiah
He is striding to Golgotha
so that we escape the fire

This triumphant, gurgling bundle,
out of an adopted womb,
leaps to Death then resurrection
via a stone hewn waiting room

Medway Romance

I didn't expect to fall in love
in the back of a Transit in Gillingham
I had not planned for an absence of forests
and street lights make feeble jewels
With love there must be words
I glided my foot towards hers
hoping she would exclaim 'sorry'
so that I could say 'not at all'
Unable to explain the thudding inside
I consulted the mind
but found it was doing pirouettes
Come back foot, that's corny
My eyes finger the dark
her face is in there somewhere
serene and tender
Love seeped in
and the only one who didn't know
was her

Raising the Dead

You do not allow for the natural end
the breath scurrying on ahead
too excited to explain where it's going
you see hearses as God giving a poor account of
    Himself
you regard grief as something Catholics do to
    themselves
you can not praise the purity of death
you do not allow for the natural end

You do not allow for the natural end
the obsolete organs swopped for singing
not heard of this side of agony
you produce pantomimes and call them triumph
you hack yourself with pristine dogma
you present Christ as a compulsive talker
you do not allow for the natural end

You do not allow for the natural end
the shattering of caskets and heaving of head stones
has not occurred to you
you practice formulas, you hit and miss
you shout at the cripple for not being healed
you have not noticed the confused ones
you do not allow for the natural end

'You Don't Know What to do When You Get Old'

In the shuffling melancholy
of life's grey haired rituals
where the misplaced pension book
routine becomes habitual
a nation of confused dissenters
huddles in the aftermath
of governmental legislation
video shops and sauna baths

Left to doze in plastic armchairs
nodding in and out of woe
hearts prepared for termination
by a babbling TV show
dignity of fading people
thin anxiety in their walk
some will freeze whilst some will fall
into repetitious talk

Soon the functional undertaker
watches yet one more last kiss
the coffin's sealed as grief consumes
there must be more to death than this.

Arc Lights in Palmers Green

(On hearing a film was being made about the life of Stevie Smith)

How would you now view the script girl
pen round her neck
clip board of meaningful directions?
I think that's who you'd be,
conscientious, yet enjoying the lark
Debating with the producer
as you did with God,
your argument singing with courteous anarchy.
I'm sure you'd adore shots of
precise avenues and stiff high streets,
you methodically mounting the stairs,
pausing half way up like a confident mouse
to check your shopping.
With you how the ordinary would be acclaimed
as you enjoyed the absurdities of a stop watch
only half bothering to time the dialogue

What Has Happened to the British Queue?

What has happened to the British queue
We've gone European, our manners have too
We rush and we crush as our hats go askew
What has happened to the British queue

What has happened to the British queue
A bald head with brylcream is an unusual view
Especially whilst waiting for a bus bound for Kew
What has happened to the British queue

What has happened to the British queue
It's close to extinction, apart from a few
Who still value good breeding and say 'after you'
But they're at the back of the British queue

And at the Beginning of Passion

And at the beginning of Passion
already burnt into his bones
the brand of nail marks
And at the beginning of Passion
already scythed into his scalp
the scars of the thorn crown
And to follow
the vulgar coronation
the spiteful crucifixion
And the reason for this slaughter
as the ears of the passive donkey
arched back like question marks
the sound of my name
and your name
on his lips

Mortal Foil

Cancer couldn't get me
Cancer wouldn't dare
Cancer doesn't scare me
Hate to lose my hair

Cancer's got no manners
Cancer lays you flat
Cancer's like aerobics
Stops you getting fat

Cancer is an addict
Cancer's full of drugs
Cancer is a tantrum
Won't respond to hugs

Cancer stalks the playgroup
Comes from who knows where
Dolly's now an orphan
Cancer isn't fair

Cancer is religious
Urges you to pray
In such numb devotion
A reverent display

Cancer is remedial
Never sees the fun
That even if it kills you
Doesn't mean it's won

Glory Train

The Bible that I read interprets poverty as sin
I'd like to prove this now but I'm not sure what
  part it's in
So if you're in a death camp, finding things a little
  tough
The reason why you're there is that your faith is not
  enough

I don't use words like failure because everything's
  so super
I know that God can heal, and if He can't there's
  always BUPA
And here I am so famous, with a world wide
  ministry
Having scrapped the bleeding Jesus for a prosperous
  Trinity

Marketable confidence and public platform charm
A rags to riches testimony, a talent to disarm
And then the big finale with a tax free loud hard sell
No need to trouble acolytes with sad rumours of a
  hell

Now all you people unemployed, no need to feel
  condemned
It's true that you're all losers, but here's how to
  make amends
Remove the truth of suffering and other dangerous
  parts
Encourage self obsession in the Rolls Royce of your
  hearts

For Valeri and His Kind

I'm waiting for my heavenly crown
Here in Gehenna's model town
Where smirking demons beat me down
And shroud me in a blood bruised gown

Where is the holy hill of Zion?
I need to kiss the hill of Zion
And hear the roar of Judah's Lion
I crave the healing earth of Zion

I lose all count of body blows
That aim, then bounce off crotch and toes
This temple pocked with electrodes
Is strewn and striped with Calvary's woes

Beyond this snow death land of spite
An empty gallows burns with might
A splayed Jew stretched out like a kite
Flew up from hell and gave me light

Where is the holy hill of Zion?
One day I'll touch the hill of Zion
And smell the mane of Judah's Lion
I suffer this because of Zion

Yule Gruel

Christmas is coming
The goose is getting fat
It's been force fed since early March
Now what d'ya think of that
If you haven't got your Barclay Card
Your Diner's Club will do
If you haven't got your Diner's Club
Poor you

Christmas comes but once a year and when it does it's
   blotto
Lurching in and reeling out of Santa Claus' grotto
Meanwhile in the food hall there are little treats to
   please us
So who's that naked, staring infant holding hands with
   Jesus?

Christmas is coming
The goose is getting fat
It's been force fed since early March
Now what d'ya think of that
If you haven't got your Barclay Card
Your Diner's Club will do
If you haven't got your Diner's Club
Poor you

H'y'ar kid now what you need's some sumptious
   Camenbert
Very big in Normandy, what happened to your hair?
German chocolates, lakes of wine and sweet liquers to
   lick
The kid's not eaten anything so why's he being sick?

Why not take a stocking back for all your hungry
   chums
Full of gooey, sticky things for stretched tight bloated
   tums
I'll spend this peaceful Christmas in a happy haze of
   cheer
And if you're still alive by then we'll celebrate New
   Year

   Christmas is coming
   The goose is getting fat
   It's been force fed since early March
   Now what d'ya think of that
   If you haven't got your Barclay Card
   Your Diner's Club will do
   If you haven't got your Diner's Club
   Poor you

It now appears that Jesus has run short of meek and
   mild
He's looking very angry as He's burying the child
And now He's pointing at me—'Look I'm not the only
   one'
'Neglect the persecuted and you do it to the Son'

   All together now . . .
   Christmas is coming . . .

Final Question

Final Question

Why on earth is an elephant
Why in sky is a cloud
Why under water is a scheming alligator
Why is man so proud